Watch Plants Grow!
WATCH PINE TREES GROW

By Therese Shea

Gareth Stevens
Publishing

Please visit our Web site, www.garethstevens.com. For a free color catalog of all our high-quality books, call toll free 1-800-542-2595 or fax 1-877-542-2596.

Library of Congress Cataloging-in-Publication Data

Shea, Therese.
Watch pine trees grow / Therese Shea.
    p. cm. – (Watch plants grow!)
 ISBN 978-1-4339-4839-8 (library binding)
 ISBN 978-1-4339-4840-4 (pbk.)
 ISBN 978-1-4339-4841-1 (6-pack)
 1. Pine–Growth–Juvenile literature. 2. Pine–Development–Juvenile literature. I. Title.
QK494.5.P66M365 2011
634.9'751–dc22

2010038502

First Editon

Published in 2011 by
Gareth Stevens Publishing
111 East 14th Street, Suite 349
New York, NY 10003

Editor: Kristen Rajczak
Designer: Haley W. Harasymiw

Photo credits: Cover, pp. 1, 3, 5, 7, 9, 13, 15, 19, 21, 23 Shutterstock.com; p. 11 © Aflo/Nature Picture Library; p. 17 Seymour Hewitt/Iconica/Getty Images.

Printed in the United States of America

CPSIA compliance information: Batch #CW11GS: For further information contact Gareth Stevens, New York, New York at 1-800-542-2595.

WATCH
PINE TREES
GROW

Pine trees grow from seeds.

5

The seeds are in cones.

Pinecones drop to the ground. Seeds fall out.

A pine tree grows.

The leaves of pine trees are long and thin.

13

Each leaf is a needle.

Pine trees are green
all year.

Paper comes from
pine trees.

People make tables from pine trees too.

21

We eat some big pine seeds. They are pine nuts.

Words to Know

cone

needle

seeds

24